CHARLES C. RYRIE
The Man, His Ministry, and His Method

Paul D. Weaver

Exegetica Publishing, 2022

Charles Ryrie was one of the kindest men I have ever known, from my Dean's office at a seminary to eating out in a restaurant with my family including my children. But it was his teaching that I knew first, in particular, his seminal work *Dispensationalism Today* (1965) which has governed my thinking about reading the Bible for over four decades. Therefore, I am elated that a small work reviewing the life of Ryrie and his theological method has been presented by Paul Weaver. This initial glimpse into this important theologian will be of benefit to seminary teachers, pastors, and laypersons, even those who disagree with Ryrie's approach. There is a clarity to the man and a clarity to Weaver's presentation of this important Bible teacher.

Dr. Mike Stallard
Director of International Ministries
Friends of Israel Gospel Ministry

Dr. Weaver's book *Charles C. Ryrie: The Man, His Ministry, and His Method* reflected the writing style of Dr. Ryrie in that the book is concise yet extremely profound. Very little has been written about this influential theologian and Dr. Weaver does an excellent job of summarizing his life, his theology, and his impact on Christianity all over the globe. I highly commend the reading of this book to everyone from lay people to scholars.

Dr. Joseph Parle
Provost and Senior Professor
College of Biblical Studies
Author of *Dispensational Development and Departure*

With relatively little written concerning the person, influence, and theological method of the significant, dispensational, theologian Charles Ryrie, this book comes with the remedy to this deficiency. Weaver has done an excellent job in describing Ryrie's life, ministry, and biblical approach (including his hermeneutic and method for systematic theology). Traditional dispensationalism is described by referring to Ryrie's own writing, books and articles that reference him, and two personal interviews that Weaver had with Ryrie. Weaver includes the various criticisms that were leveled against Ryrie and Ryrie's own responses to such critiques. This is an easy read, but full of personal and helpful insights into this great theologian, administrator, and professor.

Dr. Stephen Bramer
Chair and Professor of Bible Exposition
Dallas Theological Seminary

Paul Weaver has performed a vital service by writing this introduction to the life and legacy of Charles Ryrie. He shows why Dr. Ryrie was one of the most important theologians of the twentieth century. As one of Dr Ryrie's students, I can attest to his influence on my life. He loved the Word of God, and he loved sharing it with others. Though Dr. Ryrie has gone to heaven, his influence lives on around the world. Read this book and see for yourself.

Dr. Ray Pritchard
President
Keep Believing Ministries

As a young man, I will never forget the privilege of listening to Dr. Ryrie's rich teaching. A gifted master teacher, Dr. Ryrie communicated complex theological issues with utter clarity, simplicity, and dry humor. In this short book, Paul Weaver not only highlights Dr. Ryrie's role as a theological pioneer and voice for conservative evangelicalism, but also shines a spotlight on his hermeneutic and theological method. A great read about a great man of God whose teachings and writings continue to influence countless lives, including mine.

Dr. Don Lough, Jr.
President & CEO
Word of Life Fellowship, Inc.

The teaching and writing of Dr. Charles Ryrie had a profound impact on an entire generation of pastors, theologians, and laypeople, including me. His concise, careful clarity on complex subjects was his hallmark. His consistent method of literal interpretation was the foundation of his understanding of God's Word and is much needed today. I'm deeply grateful to Paul for keeping Dr. Ryrie's life and legacy alive for another generation.

Dr. Mark Hitchcock
Senior Pastor, Faith Bible Church, Edmond, OK
Research Professor of Bible Exposition
Dallas Theological Seminary

CHARLES C. RYRIE
The Man, His Ministry, and His Method

Paul D. Weaver

Exegetica Publishing, 2022

This writing was originally published in the Fall 2013 issue of the
Journal of Ministry and Theology, a ministry of Baptist Bible Seminary
(Clarks Summit, PA).

For information visit: www.weaverwebpage.org

Acknowledgements

I am thankful to Dr. Gary Gromacki and Dr. Michael Stallard, formerly co-editors of the *Journal of Theology and Ministry* for choosing to include the original work as an article in the before mentioned journal. I am indebted to Dr. Stallard, for his course "Advanced Theological Method," which led me down this road of investigation. I am greatly appreciative of my wife, who proofread this manuscript and encouraged me from the inception of this project.

Finally, I am thankful to Dr. Charles Ryrie, who invested hours of time fielding my many questions during the course of our interviews, email conversations, other correspondences.

Since the initial writing of this content, Charles Ryrie entered into the presence of his Savior on February 16, 2016.

Dedication

*To Dr. Charles Caldwell Ryrie (1925–2016) who has left
an indelible mark on my spiritual and theological
development and that of countless others.*

CONTENTS

INTRODUCTION

If one were asked to list the most influential theologians of the twentieth century, certain scholars would be sure to make the cut. Charles C. Ryrie is one such theologian. Walter Elwell would certainly agree. In his edited work, *Elwell's Handbook of Evangelical Theologians*, Ryrie is included as one of the thirty-three most influential theologians of the twentieth century.[1] He has indeed had a sizable influence on the broader evangelical movement in general, conservative evangelicalism in particular, and has had an even greater sway upon evangelicals who are dispensational.

Need for this Study

Ryrie's influence in American evangelicalism has certainly been felt, but his impact is not limited to North America. By virtue of the students he has taught, who teach and preach in nearly every country of the world, and the books that he has written which have been translated into a multitude of languages,[2] his impact has been felt globally. Apart from a few relatively brief biographical sketches, little has been written about him and even less about his theological method. These factors warrant further investigation into the life, writings, hermeneutic, and theological method of the theologian, Charles Caldwell Ryrie.

---

[1] Ellwell, Walter, ed. *Handbook of Evangelical Theologians* (Grand Rapids: Baker), 1993.

[2] *Basic Theology* alone has been translated into twenty-one languages.

Purpose for this Study

The purpose of this study is not merely to write a biographical sketch of the life of Ryrie, or even to understand his body of work (although this paper will certainly attempt to do both). This book will seek to investigate the life and writings of Charles C. Ryrie with the purpose of understanding the hermeneutic he used, and the theological method[3] he implemented, resulting in the theological system for which he is famous.

Method of this Study

This study will begin with an investigation into the formative years of Ryrie's childhood, his education, and the influential figures in his life. Next, an examination of the important roles in which Ryrie functioned will take place. He will be examined from the standpoint of a tenured professor, prolific writer, bold pioneer, ardent apologist, and ordained minister. After such a study is complete, a discussion of his pre-understandings will be included and special attention given to his hermeneutical principles. Consideration will also be given to his integration of the Old and New Testaments. Space will then be devoted to Ryrie's integration of biblical truth with other academic disciplines, followed by an analysis of possible interpretive motifs employed by Ryrie and a defense given for the one in which this writer believes is most reflected in his writings. Ryrie's views on the related disciplines of biblical studies will be addressed, and this will conclude with a summary section that

---

[3] Theological method is a process implemented (whether intentional or non-intentional) that results in the development of theological beliefs. A good theological method provides criteria to validate that process.

articulates Ryrie's theological method as perceived by this writer.

THE MAN

It is incredible that so many systematic theologies have been read without the reader knowing much about the authors' personal lives. It seems only logical that prior to reading a theological work, one would want to better understand the theologian behind it. For good or bad, humans are a composite of our experiences, culture, teachers, and influencers. While some theologians are able to move beyond the views handed down to them, others are not. Still others are fortunate to have been handed down a truly biblical framework and are able to build on such a foundation and advance that theological system. Ryrie is one such theologian. Ryrie's strong theological heritage set him on solid ground to take evangelicalism and more specifically dispensational evangelicalism onward. To understand Ryrie's theological method, it is of special worth and interest to study the most formative years and experiences in his life.

His Early Life

Charles Ryrie was born into the God-fearing home of John Alexander and Elizabeth Caldwell Ryrie in 1925. Ryrie was raised in Alton, Illinois, a town located just across the Mississippi River from the city of St. Louis (where he was born). His father was a banker, and Charles believed he would continue the family banking business one day, but God had other plans. Young Ryrie was a fifth generation attendee of the First

Baptist Church of Alton, Illinois.[4] This church was a member of a denomination that is now known as American Baptist. It was here, at the age of five, that Ryrie came to faith in Jesus Christ. Ryrie recollects concerning his church experience, "It was not liberal but not particularly deep."[5] When asked if First Baptist Alton had a futuristic interpretation of Scripture, Ryrie stated that it did; however, "Prophecy was incidental. No particular doctrine stands out."[6]

In 1942, at the young age of sixteen, Ryrie graduated from high school, just six weeks following the attack on Pearl Harbor. He was the valedictorian of his class and earned a 96.8 grade point average.[7] Despite young Ryrie being the valedictorian, his father felt he still needed to improve upon his study skills prior to his entrance into college. At his father's direction, Ryrie attended a boarding school for one semester—Stony Brook School in Long Island, New York.[8] Frank Gaebelein, editor of *Our Hope* magazine, and son of Arno Gaebelein,[9] was the headmaster at Stony Brook.

---

[4] Darrell Goemaat and Kevin Mungons, "Have Something to Say, and Say It Clearly," *Baptist Bulletain,* accessed October 12, 2012, http://baptistbulletin.org/?p=1347.

[5] Charles C. Ryrie, telephone interview with the author of this work, November 6, 2012.

[6] Charles C. Ryrie, telephone interview with the author of this work, November 6, 2012.

[7] Darrell Goemaat and Kevin Mungons, "Have Something to Say, and Say It Clearly" http://baptistbulletin.org/?p=1347.

[8] Stony Brook School was an all boys college prep school, established in 1922 with the motto "Character before Career," accessed, November 16, 2012, www.stonybrookschool.org/about/school-mission. It has since chosen to admit female students as well.

[9] Arno Gaebelein was a prominent prophecy speaker and dispensationalist. He was also the Associate Editor of the Scofield Reference Bible and editor of *Our Hope* magazine, which his son Frank

His Higher Education

After a semester of studies at Stony Brook, at Gaebelein's recommendation, Ryrie followed in the footsteps of his older brother and enrolled at Haverford College, located just outside of Philadelphia, Pennsylvania. Haverford was a Quaker school. It was there that Ryrie enrolled in the mathematics program with a view to enter into the banking business upon graduation. He was planning to begin his professional career at his family's bank.[10]

After a conversation with Lewis Sperry Chafer, Ryrie's life direction dramatically changed from banking to full-time Christian service. Prior to graduating from Haverford, Ryrie applied and was accepted at Dallas Theological Seminary (DTS). Enns states in his short biography of Ryrie, "After attending Dallas for two years he petitioned Haverford to grant him his diploma on the basis of his studies at Dallas. (Haverford had made similar allowances for medical students). Haverford

---

edited thereafter. Scofield has been given much credit for popularizing dispensationalism, via his study Bible. Yet, a reading of personal correspondences between Arno Gaebelein and Scofield points to Gaebelein as the source of much of its eschatological content. Scofield writes to Gaebelein, "My beloved Brother: By all means follow your own views of prophetic analysis. I sit at your feet when it comes to prophecy and congratulate in advance the future readers of the Reference Bible on having in their hands a safe, clear, sane guide through what to most is a labrynth." (letter, dated April 29, 1931; quoted in Michael Stallard, *The Early Twentieth-Century Dispensationalism of Arno C. Gaebelein*, [Lewiston, NY: Edwin Mellin, 2002], 99). Ryrie recalls just once having heard Arno speak at the commencement service of Stony Brook (phone interview, November 6, 2012). While Ryrie did not sit under the teaching of Arno personally, he certainly was influenced by this early and influential dispensationalist through the teaching he passed on to his son Frank.

[10] *This is Dallas* 46, no. 1 (Jan./Feb., 1970), unnumbered pages 3–4.

agreed, conferring the baccalaureate degree in June 1946; and Dallas Seminary awarded him a Th.M. in May 1947."[11]

Ryrie's Th.M. thesis was entitled, "The Relation of the New Covenant to Premillennialism." His Th.D. dissertation would later build upon the foundation of this study.

Having a great respect for the scholarship of Carl F. Henry, who came from the Northern Baptist denomination himself, and understanding the benefits of obtaining advanced degrees from different institutions, Ryrie began to make plans to study at Northern Baptist Theological Seminary. Henry eventually departed from this denominational school (due to its liberal trajectory) to join others in founding Fuller Seminary in Pasadena, California. Due to the uncertainty of who would replace Henry, Ryrie chose instead to return to DTS and work on a Th.D.[12] Ryrie completed his Th.D. in 1949. His dissertation was titled and later published as, *The Basis of the Premillennial Faith.*

Ryrie's studies did not stop at this terminal degree. He also earned a Ph.D. from the University of Edinburgh. There he studied under notable scholars, among others, J. H. S. Burleigh, Matthew Black, and Thomas Torrance.[13] Burleigh and Black

---

[11] Paul P. Enns, "Charles Ryrie," in *Handbook of Evangelical Theologians* (Grand Rapids: Baker, 1993). In Logos Bible Software.

[12] Ryrie, interview, November 6, 2012.

[13] Thomas Torrance was an ordained minister in the Church of Scotland and is regarded by some as one of the most important theologians of the twentieth century. Torrance studied under Karl Barth and built upon Barth's views.

During Ryrie's Ph.D. studies he was exposed to pure Barthianism straight from one of Barth's own students. Rather than becoming a follower of Barth himself, Ryrie became more convinced of his own understanding. It was this exposure to Neo-Orthodoxy that led Ryrie to write, *Neo-Orthodoxy: What it is, and what it does* (Chicago: Moody,

served as advisors in his dissertation work.[14] Interestingly, his dissertation topic was one of particular interest to conservatives but was read, advised, and accepted by relatively liberal professors. One notable instance that illustrates these professors' liberal leanings was the request of Black, done in a gracious manner: "Rather than writing 'the Bible says,' would you be willing instead to write, 'Paul says?'"[15] Ryrie acquiesced to this request since (1) it did not require any compromise of his theological position, and (2) it was an accurate statement. Ryrie earned his Ph.D. in 1954. His dissertation was later published by Moody in 1970 as *The Role of Women in the Church*.[16]

1956). Ryrie writes, "Too few conservative pastors and laymen have been able to study something concise, non-technical, but accurate on this subject" (*Neo-Orthodoxy*, 10). In this book Ryrie helps the pastor and lay person alike understand the complexities and pitfalls of neo-orthodoxy. Ryrie did not pull any punches. In one place he states concerning neo-orthodoxy, "A theological hoax—that's how one might describe Barthinianism...It has been hailed as the new or neo-orthodoxy; in reality it is nothing but a false or pseudo-orthodoxy" (*Neo-orthodoxy*, 9–10). It is important to note that Ryrie was untouched by the destructive teachings of Torrence and other liberal scholars under whom he studied for his Ph.D. Ryrie's theological foundation had already been well established and therefore he successfully navigated through the waters of liberalism without being shipwrecked by them. For these reasons, it is notable that none of the before mentioned scholars of Edinburgh will be listed amongst the most influential or even secondary influencers upon the life and theology of Charles C. Ryrie.

[14] Charles C. Ryrie, *The Role of Women in the Church,* 2nd ed. (Nashville: B & H Publishing Academic, 2011), xv.

[15] This is a paraphrase by Ryrie from his recollection of a discussion he had with Matthew Black. Ryrie repeated this conversation that he had with Matthew Black. Ryrie repeated this conversation that he had with Black in a personal phone interview conducted with the writer of this paper on November 6, 2012.

[16] This book was first published by MacMillan, later it was printed by Moody Press, but currently rights are owned by Broadman and Holman Publishing Group where it remains in print since 2011.

Influential Individuals in the Life of Ryrie

Every prominent theologian in history is regarded as significant because their teachings, writings, speeches, sermons, and/or personal conversations have in one way or another had a profound impact on the lives of their students, readers, and acquaintances. In the same way, theologians have been impacted through not only events, books, and educational institutions, but people. Ryrie is no exception. Key individuals in Ryrie's life had a profound impact upon him and his theology. They served as role models, confidants, teachers, and guides to help in the formation of Charles Ryrie, the theologian. Three primary influencers will be discussed in greater detail, and three secondary influencers will be referenced in a more cursory manner.

The Influence of Ryrie's Father

Mr. Ryrie, Charles's father, played a significant part in the spiritual birth, growth, and guidance of his two sons. He led both Charles and his brother to the Lord. Ryrie does not recall whether he was in kindergarten or the first grade, when in his own words, "We had just started school, and we were at home at the time, and there is no question in my mind that was the time I received the Lord."[17] Ryrie's father taught a Sunday school class, and for a while he was also a Sunday school superintendent. Speaking respectfully of his father, Ryrie states, "Looking back, I believe he was a Spirit—capital 'S,' self—small 's,' taught person of the Bible... He read the right books...Chafer was a big influence in his life...Most of his spiritual growth was as an adult."[18] Ryrie, the father, also

---

[17] Ryrie, interview, November 6, 2012.
[18] Ryrie, interview, November 6, 2012.

taught a home-based Bible class, "before they were popular."[19] Even as a child Charles had an aptitude for learning and a desire to understand the deeper truths of Scripture. Ryrie recalls,

> Once in a while, if I promised to obey, I was allowed to sit in on the home [Bible] class...I remember once he [Ryrie the elder] was teaching that little book by Scofield called, *Rightly Dividing the Word of Truth*, it had not only eschatology in it, but the two natures, judgment...I do remember sitting in on some of the nights where he was teaching that book.[20]

There can be no doubt that Ryrie's early years were heavily influenced by his father, his teachings, his modeling, and certainly his guidance.

The Influence of Frank Gaebelein

As mentioned previously, Charles Ryrie spent one semester at Stony Brook School to prepare for college. It was here that Ryrie came into contact with Frank Gaebelein, the founder and headmaster of the school.[21] Gaebelein also had a significant impact on Ryrie. Gaebelein taught Romans, a senior-level Bible class. When asked if Gaebelein had a significant influence upon him, Ryrie stated, "Oh yes...Dr. Frank Gaebelein was very involved with us students. It was only a male school in those days...Dr. Gaebelein taught senior Bible, he taught the book of

---

[19] Ryrie, interview, November 6, 2012.

[20] Ryrie, interview, November 6, 2012.

[21] Cheryl L. Fawcett and Jamie Thompson, "Frank E. Gaebelein," accessed November 16, 2012, http://www2.talbot.edu/ce20/educators/view.cfm?n=frank_gaebelein#bibliography.

Romans and I remember a lot from that class...He always presided and often spoke in chapel."[22] Ryrie also recalls correspondence with Gaebelein which was the impetus for his writing of *Dispensationalism Today:*

> In the 60's the Scofield Bible was being revised; Dr. Gaebelein was the editor. He wrote me a letter. I was at Dallas at that time. [This was during his first stint as a professor of theology, prior to becoming president of Philadelphia College of Bible, which is now called Cairn University.] He said, "I think you should write a book on Dispensationalism. The Scofield Bible revision will be out and it would be great to have around the same time a book like that." He said, "I will promise to write the foreword." So, that is what really urged me to write what was called *Dispensationalism Today*. It came out before the [New] Scofield Reference Bible because the Scofield was delayed. He wrote the foreword, and of course it was revised and is now just called *Dispensationalism*. But he had a major part in that.[23]

Gaebelein influenced Ryrie in the classroom as a teenager, advised him in selecting a college, and years later encouraged Ryrie to write what would amount to be, one of the most important and influential books on the subject of dispensationalism.

---

[22] Ryrie, interview, November 6, 2012.
[23] Ryrie, interview, November 6, 2012.

The Influence of Lewis Sperry Chafer

While Gaebelein certainly had a significant influence upon Ryrie early on and years later, there was another man who had an even more profound impact upon Ryrie and his theology than Gaebelein. That man was Lewis Sperry Chafer. Chafer's contact with Ryrie and influence was over a long period of time. Chafer's influence on Ryrie was not limited to his seminary years, but also during his college years, as a teenager at Stony Brook, and even as a young child.

As a Child

Ryrie's grandfather, a widower, lived with Ryrie's family when Ryrie was a child. Lewis Sperry Chafer was friends with Ryrie's grandfather. When Chafer would come to speak at a Brethren assembly in St. Louis, [24] he would often stay in their home. Ryrie fondly recalls his early memories of the Chafers, "He was quite a musician. He was a tenor; Mrs. Chafer was an alto. I do have vivid memories of the two of them sitting at a piano in my folk's home and singing duets."[25] From a very early age, Ryrie was exposed to one of the great movers and shakers of evangelicalism. When asked by this writer, if he understood the significance of having Chafer in his home, Ryrie responded, "Yes, I had an appreciation and knowledge for who he was, I think very much so."[26] From a very early age, Ryrie was influenced by some great minds and dispensational teachers of the Bible. It is also interesting to note, that at the time of his ordination, when asked by those sitting on his ordination council

---

[24] Darrell Goemaat and Kevin Mungons, "Have Something to Say." http://baptistbulletin.org/?p=1347.

[25] Ryrie, interview, November 6, 2012.

[26] Ryrie, interview, November 6, 2012.

why he attended DTS[27] he answered, "I didn't know of any other seminary."[28] Although, a member of a Northern Baptist Church (a denomination known today as American Baptist), Ryrie was so influenced by Chafer, Scofield, and other dispensationalist teachers that Dallas Theological Seminary was the only seminary he considered.

As a Teenager

The influence of Chafer continued beyond Ryrie's childhood. As referenced above, Ryrie's father enrolled Charles at Stony Brook School for a semester. Chafer, because of his prominence in the evangelical community, received an invitation from Stony Brook School to attend its graduation ceremony. Ryrie surmises that Chafer must have thought he personally sent the invitation.[29] In response to what Chafer thought was an invitation directly from young Ryrie, Chafer wrote a personal letter to Ryrie which included an encouragement about ministry involvement, "I don't know what you are going to do with your life, but there is not much competition in the field of having experts in the knowledge of the Word of God."[30] Although, this was not the time Ryrie committed to full-time Christian service, Chafer's words left a strong impression upon young Ryrie.[31]

---

[27] The question implied some dissatisfaction that he did not attend a Northern Baptist denominational school, of which the church was a member.

[28] Ryrie, interview, November 6, 2012.

[29] Ryrie, interview, November 6, 2012.

[30] Ryrie, interview, November 6, 2012.

[31] Ryrie, interview, November 6, 2012.

As a College Student

Ryrie stated, "Chafer is the reason I am in the ministry."[32] It was a personal meeting with Chafer at the request of Charles Ryrie that would be life-changing and would redirect the course of Ryrie's life. While Ryrie was attending Haverford College, he read in the local paper that Chafer was nearby, conducting a week-long series of messages at a church in the area. Ryrie went to hear Chafer speak, hoping to arrange some personal time with him. After the Sunday night service, Ryrie approached Chafer and asked if he had some time to talk. Chafer agreed. Later in the week, they met at the hotel in which Chafer was staying, the Robert Morris Hotel, in downtown Philadelphia. Ryrie stated, "That night I felt a call to ministry...we talked and prayed. I date that night as two things, a dedication of life and call to Christian service."[33] That was April 23, 1943.

As a Seminary Student

While Chafer invested into many young men who were training for ministry, few, if any, had a longer history than Ryrie had with Chafer. Despite this fact, Ryrie recalls, "we were all Chafer's boys and as much as possible we were treated as such."[34] While at DTS, Ryrie sat under the teaching of Lewis Sperry Chafer. In his words, "I was influenced on his position and insistence on grace and grace alone."[35] Ryrie remarked that one of the predominant teachings of Chafer was in the area of grace. What do his former students remember about his

---

[32] Ryrie, interview, November 6, 2012.

[33] Ryrie, interview, November 6, 2012.

[34] Ryrie, interview, November 6, 2012.

[35] Charles C. Ryrie, Video interview, Evangelical Free Alliance, accessed October 13, 2012, http://vimeo.com/19816195.

teaching? "Almost anyone who had him as a teacher, what would they answer, almost uniformly grace."[36] Chafer's teaching and insistence upon grace can be evidenced in many of Ryrie's later writings.[37]

The Influence of Various Other Individuals

John Alexander Ryrie, Frank Gaebelein, and Lewis Sperry Chafer all had a profound impact upon the spiritual formation, biblical foundation, hermeneutical understanding, and theological method of Charles C. Ryrie. They, by far, had the most significant influence upon Ryrie, the theologian. Yet, Ryrie cites three other individuals who had an important influence upon his life.

While in college Ryrie would often take the train into Philadelphia to sit under the teaching of the famous Presbyterian dispensationalist, Donald Grey Barnhouse. Barnhouse was the pastor of the Tenth Presbyterian Church.[38] The teachings of Barnhouse added to Ryrie's dispensational understanding of Scripture.[39]

---

[36] Ibid.

[37] While these teachings are prominent in many of Ryrie's writings, it is most noticeable in his books, *The Grace of God, Balancing the Christian Life*, (especially chapters four and seventeen, "The Old and the New," and "Must Christ be Lord to Be Savior?"), and in his book, *So Great a Salvation.*

[38] Ryrie, interview, November 9, 2012.

[39] By the time Ryrie exited his teenage years he had already been influenced by three very prominent dispensationalists: Chafer, Gaebelein, and Barnhouse and two of the most important dispensationalists of the early twentieth century: Lewis S. Chafer and Arno Gaebelein (through the teachings of his son, Frank). Ryrie had the perfect theological pedigree to eventually become one of the foremost defenders and articulators of dispensationalism.

While President of Philadelphia College of Bible, Clarence Mason, Dean and Professor, was a great source of help and encouragement to Ryrie. In a lighthearted manner, Ryrie stated, "I don't think I would have survived without his help."[40]

A third notable figure was the famous preacher and friend W. A. Criswell. Criswell was an influential Southern Baptist and a dispensational premillennialist. Ryrie attended and taught at First Baptist Dallas, where Criswell pastored for nearly fifty years.

---

[40] Ryrie, interview, November 9, 2012.

HIS MINISTRY

Charles Ryrie had a long and influential academic and ministerial career that spanned several decades and has had a lasting impact. His influence was significant and opportunities of ministry varied. He taught at five institutions (four of higher education as well as one church). As a young man he became president of a Bible college, yet he is most noted for his prolific writing career, in which he was both a pioneer in many of his writings as well as an apologist defending various positions of theology.

Ryrie, the Professor and President

Ryrie began his academic career the summer following his graduation from DTS with a Th.M. He taught that first summer at Midwest Bible and Missionary Institute.[41] In 1949, after completing his Th.D. at DTS, Ryrie was invited to teach at Westmont College and eventually became the Department Chairman of Biblical Studies and Philosophy.[42] Ryrie went there to teach Bible and mathematics. When he arrived he was made Associate Professor of Greek and Bible. In 1950 the president was dismissed. Two-thirds of the faculty tried to force the board to keep the president. Although Ryrie felt pressured, he did not

---

[41] Midwest Bible and Missionary Institute was one of the colleges that would eventually merge to form Calvary Bible College known today as Calvary University (Kansas City, MO), accessed September 19, 2022, https://www.calvary.edu/history/.

[42] This was a professional advancement opportunity for Ryrie that developed out of an unfortunate faculty departure.

join the dissenting faculty.[43] The teachers involved were terminated by the board. To fill the void felt by this large departure, Ryrie took on the additional responsibilities of Dean of Men and Chairman of the Department of Biblical Studies and Philosophy.[44]

Shortly after the death of Chafer (Ryrie's mentor), Ryrie was invited to teach at DTS as a part-time faculty member. During this time he was also completing his Ph.D. dissertation. This part-time position developed into a full-time position on the faculty of the Systematic Theology Department. Ryrie remained at DTS for five years, when he accepted the invitation to become the president of Philadelphia College of Bible.[45] Ryrie was just thirty-three years of age when he accepted this position. He remained president until 1962. When asked how he would describe this time period in his ministry, Ryrie stated, "A very happy time. I liked teaching college age kids. I liked teaching them because that is where many of them are making many life decisions."[46] Ryrie made it a personal goal to speak once a week in chapel unless he was out of town. His book *Making the Most of Life*, was the work product of those chapel messages.

In 1962, Ryrie returned to Dallas Theological Seminary to become the Chairman of Systematic Theology and the first Dean of Doctoral Studies. Ryrie retired in 1983, and until recently, continued to teach as an adjunct faculty member at various schools, as well as a guest speaker in churches and conferences around the world.

---

[43] Ryrie, interview, November 9, 2012.

[44] Enns, *Handbook of Evangelical Theologians*, electronic edition.

[45] Which changed its name to Philadelphia Biblical University and is now called Cairn University.

[46] Ryrie, interview, November 9, 2012.

Ryrie, the Prolific Writer

Charles Ryrie has written a total of thirty-two books that have sold more than 1.5 million copies worldwide.[47] This does not include the Ryrie Study Bible which has sold 2.6 million copies alone.[48] In an interview with the *Baptist Bulletin* when asked, "How did you develop your ability to explain things in simple language that a layperson can understand?" Ryrie responded, "It's the way the gift of teaching or exhortation is worked out in me: conciseness...On the human side, I think it is because off and on through the years, I've taught children."[49]

Not only is Ryrie a prolific writer, but his writings are diverse in their scope. As one might expect of a professor of Systematic Theology, Ryrie has written the most in this area.

- *Basic Theology*
- *Survey of Bible Doctrine*
- *Dispensationalism; The Holy Spirit*
- *Come Quickly Lord Jesus*
- *The Best is Yet to Come*
- *The Basis of the Premillennial Faith*
- *The Final Countdown*
- *What You Should Know About the Rapture*

He has also written in the area of contemporary issues.

- *The Role of Women in the Church*

---

[47] John D. Hannah, *An Uncommon Union: Dallas Theological Seminary and American Evangelicalism* (Grand Rapids: Zondervan), 264.

[48] James Vincent, *The MBI Story: The Vision and Worldwide Impact of Moody Bible Institute* (Chicago: Moody Publishers, 2011), np.

[49] Darrell Goemaat and Kevin Mungons, "Have Something to Say" http://baptistbulletin.org/?p=1347.

- *Neo-Orthodoxy*
- *What You Should Know About Social Responsibility*
- *Biblical Answers to Tough Questions*
- *Biblical Answers to Contemporary Issues.*

Ryrie composed exegetical works and commentaries as well.

- *Thessalonians*
- *Acts*
- *Revelation*
- *The Miracles of Our Lord*

He has written in the area of Christian living

- *Balancing the Christian Life*
- *Making the Most of life*

He contributed to a history of the English Bible, *Let It Go Among Our People.* He has also written a handful of works of a very practical nature including two books on object lessons, a book about sitting on a non-profit board, and a book about communicating Bible doctrine in practical manner. He has even written what is classified as juvenile reading: *The Young Christian's Introduction to the Bible.* Ryrie has written in seven vastly different areas, and his impact with the pen is immeasurable.

In an academic world where many professors are most concerned with acceptance amongst their peers, Ryrie wrote at a level understandable by academics, pastors, and laypeople. He never lost sight of the fact, that although we need strong academicians, seminaries and Bible colleges are intended to train leaders of the church. His *Basic Theology* textbook has been translated into twenty-one different languages and is still used in Bible institutes, colleges, and seminaries around the world.

When discussing the creation of the *Ryrie Study Bible*, Ryrie states, "When I was working on the Study Bible, I thought of the people in home Bible classes."[50] The *Ryrie Study Bible* was finished in 1978 and then revised with two thousand additional notes in 1995. When Ryrie first began his interest in writing, he asked Philip Howard, the editor of *Sunday School Times,* "Dr. Howard, how do you learn to write?" The answer to this question would stay with Ryrie. Howard stated, "Have something to say and say it clearly." Paul Enns writes, "Dr. Ryrie is especially gifted in his ability to clarify profound theological truths in simple precise language. He has enabled people to understand biblical truth that they would otherwise not readily comprehend and in this he has made an inestimable contribution to the Christian world."[51]

This is also evidenced in Ryrie's own words, concerning the need for popular-level writings on Neo-orthodoxy, "The difficulty is that too few conservative pastors and laymen have been able to study something concise, nontechnical, but accurate on this subject. To help meet this need is the purpose of this book."[52]

Ryrie's writings are characterized by not only clarity but also charity. In the same work just referenced, Ryrie states, "May God give us discernment of the issues at stake, clear

---

[50] Darrell Goemaat and Kevin Mungons, "Have Something to Say, and Say It Clearly" http://baptistbulletin.org/?p=1347.

[51] Paul P. Enns, "Charles Ryrie," in *Dictionary of Premillennial Theology,* ed. Mal Couch (Grand Rapids: Kregal Publications, 1996), 67.

[52] Charles C. Ryrie, *Neo-orthodoxy: What It Is and What It Does* (Chicago: Moody, 1956), 10.

understanding for the truth, wholehearted committal to the authority of the Bible, God's Word, and deep conviction of heart to speak the truth in love."[53] Ryrie's writings always come across with kindness. One example can be found when he references the convoluted thinking in gospel tracts, "I list them without documentation since the point is not who said these but what was said, and to illustrate how varied and confusing these statements are."[54] The clearest example of charity in his writings is regarding the Lordship Salvation debate. While John MacArthur and Zane Hodges continually list names and groups, mischaracterize each other, make straw-man arguments, and overstate their own arguments, Ryrie refrains from such behavior. Unless one reads the endnotes, the reader is not likely to know that there is even a debate taking place. Even when Ryrie is diametrically opposed to a particular view, and the stakes are high, he still maintains his composure and even presents his opponents positively. Ryrie characterizes Barth as one of "Christian Gentlemen" and points to the good that he has done as well as the bad.[55]

Ryrie, the Pioneer

Ryrie had a great knack for sensing what evangelicalism required. He wrote several works that blazed a new trail or met a pressing need, sometimes even before that need surfaced. Ryrie's Ph.D. work on the subject of women's role in the church is a case-in-point. Dorothy Patterson also recognizes this aspect to Ryrie's ministry in her foreword of Ryrie's book. She states,

---

[53] Ryrie, *Neo-orthodoxy*, 62.

[54] Charles C. Ryrie, *So Great a Salvation: What It Means to Believe In Jesus Christ* (Wheaton, IL: Victor, 1989), 23.

[55] Ryrie, *Neo-orthodoxy*, 21–24.

"Again, Ryrie finds himself in the role of a prophetic scholar engaging in cutting-edge debate over a question that really had not been asked when he first penned this work as his doctoral dissertation in the mid-twentieth century, nor was the issue really of importance when Moody Publishers first issued his monograph on the subject."[56]

Ryrie's *Dispensationalism Today,* written in 1965, was also a significant groundbreaking work that helped define the term dispensationalism and respond to many false characterizations of it. It has become a classic and is still the go-to reference work on the subject.

The *Ryrie Study Bible* is another example of a work that set the stage and tone for generations to come. Ryrie wrote his study Bible prior to the popularity of study Bibles. At the time there were just a handful of options; now there are hundreds of varieties, but only a few that have sold more in number than the *Ryrie Study Bible.*

Ryrie's work on neo-orthodoxy was a work done at a popular level. Ryrie saw the great need of providing answers to the questions surfacing not only in academia but in the church at large. Ryrie was indeed a pioneer in many of the subjects in which he wrote.

Ryrie, the Apologist

Ryrie's writing career often involved defending orthodox positions and dispensational perspectives. He became an able spokesman and apologist of conservative evangelicalism in responding to the teachings of neo-orthodoxy and the inerrancy of Scripture. He became the defender of the historical

---

[56] Dorothy Patterson, foreword to *The Role of Women in the Church,* Charles Ryrie (Nashville: B & H Academic, 2011), xii.

understanding of women's role in the church. Ryrie wrote to guard against abuses of the gospel. He became the capable representative of historic dispensationalism. He also became an ardent defender of a plain interpretation of Scripture, which has a wide range of implications relating to creationism, Israel, the church, the covenants, and prophetic literature, just to name a few.

In several of his writings, Ryrie lists arguments made against his views and systematically rebuts them. In *Inerrancy* Ryrie lists three "excuses" against inerrancy.[57] In *So Great a Salvation*, he speaks of "straw men arguments,"[58] and in *Dispensationalism* he speaks of the many different "attacks" of those opposing dispensationalism.[59] Ryrie engages in issues that he deems especially important with wide-ranging implications. When he saw a lot at stake, he stepped in to provide clarity of the real issues and a defense of his positions from a biblical perspective, built upon a high view of Scripture. Regarding inerrancy, he gives the analogy of dominoes. He believes if inerrancy is "knocked over" it will have a huge "domino effect."[60]

Ryrie responds with a very serious and strong tone to those views outside of orthodoxy, because he recognizes the threat level to be great. Ryrie recognized neo-orthodoxy as a clear and present danger to evangelicalism. This is seen in his statement, "A theological hoax—that's how one might describe Barthianism that theology which calls men to the Word of God, stemmed from the writings of Barth and Brunner."[61] Ryrie sounds the alarm

---

[57] Charles C. Ryrie, *What You Should Know About Inerrancy* (Chicago: Moody Press, 1981), 21–26.

[58] Ryrie, *So Great a Salvation*, 29–33.

[59] Ryrie, *Dispensationalism* (Chicago: Moody, 1995), 12–16.

[60] Ryrie, *What You Should Know About Inerrancy*, 9–11.

[61] Ryrie, *Neo-orthodoxy*, 9.

and proclaims the dangers of what he calls a "false or pseudo-orthodoxy."[62] Ryrie also records the pervading influence of barthianism/neo-orthodoxy in seminaries and as a result, churches pastored by graduates of such seminaries. He states, "Too many are too quick to whitewash schools and men who still speak of regeneration, inspiration, the authority of the Word, etc., and too few have investigated what is really meant by those terms. The danger of such is like quicksand."[63] Ryrie points out that the danger of neo-evangelicalism is even greater because within it is some good along with the bad: "But it is this good which is like a smoke screen to some evangelicals, and there is abroad the feeling that perhaps, after all, Barthianism isn't so bad, and we shouldn't criticize it so harshly because it has done some good."[64] Ryrie points out the great dangers neo-orthodoxy does to Scripture, "The damage that liberalism has done to the Bible can never be estimated, and this is what neo-orthodoxy sides with."[65]

As an apologist Ryrie does a masterful job of pointing out fallacious logic. This can be seen in his work on neo-orthodoxy.

[neo-orthodoxy] speaks of important and real truths about God, sin, man, and the cross. But, because of neo-orthodoxy's acceptance of the liberal view of the Scriptures, the truths are based on nothing more than good stories, which may contain a grain of truth, but which also are greatly embellished. Original sin is the truest thing in the world, but the account of it in Genesis

---

[62] Ryrie, *Neo-orthodoxy*, 10.

[63] Ryrie, *Neo-orthodoxy*.

[64] Ryrie, *Neo-orthodoxy*.

[65] Ryrie, *Neo-orthodoxy*, 45.

is only a story. The resurrection of Christ is the truest thing in the world, but the Gospel accounts of it are: hopelessly garbled. Christ is the Bread of Life, but of course, not one word of the Gospel of John is historical.[66]

Ryrie is also skillful in synthesizing the theological teachings of others in an understandable fashion, and then explaining the dangers that may result. Continuing with neo-orthodoxy as an example, "To sum up: their doctrine includes orthodox terminology built on liberal exegesis; it attempts to have inspiration without infallibility, and authority without actuality. What kind of Bible is that?"[67]

Ryrie, the Ordained Minister

Charles Ryrie was ordained by the First Baptist Church of Alton, Illinois in 1947. This was the church where he grew up and his parents attended until 1949. His parents eventually left that church over the fundamentalist-modernist controversy.[68] They joined Brown Street Baptist Church, which was a member of the General Association of Regular Baptists. Much of John and Elizabeth Ryrie's Sunday school class left with them.

While Ryrie's greatest influence was with the pen, he also had a substantial ministry at First Baptist Church in Dallas,

---

[66] Ryrie, *Neo-orthodoxy*, 60.

[67] Ryrie, *Neo-orthodoxy*, 48.

[68] This was a debate beginning in the 1920's within Presbyterian and Baptist denominations. The modernists were suggesting conservatives should be more tolerant of liberal views regarding: inerrancy, the virgin birth, substitutionary atonement, Christ's bodily resurrection, and the second coming of the Lord (among others). The fundamentalists were not willing to compromise on these areas which are fundamentals of the faith, and the foundation of Orthodox Christianity.

Texas, as well as an itinerate preaching/teaching ministry in various churches around the United States. Ryrie taught a Sunday school class of over one hundred.[69] Before each quarter he would also teach the curriculum to the other Sunday school teachers. At one point, he also conducted a junior church, but not in the sense that most think of it today. It was a church for teenagers who were in the ninth through twelfth grades. They had a separate service for these young people. For a while, he was teaching two to three hundred teenagers. During this time Ryrie did not do much traveling. However, upon retirement from DTS he had more opportunities to preach and teach in the United States and in the church abroad.

---

[69] *This is Dallas* 46, no. 1 (Jan./Feb., 1970), unnumbered pages 3–4.

HIS METHOD

In his book *First Theology,* Kevin J. Vanhoozer addresses the question of which doctrine(s) should come first in the study of systematic theology. Does the study of the doctrine of God take priority, or should the doctrine of the Bible be primary? What is "first theology"? Vanhoozer states, "It is difficult to talk of God without appealing to the Bible, just as it is difficult to treat the Bible as Scripture without appealing to God."[70] Vanhoozer goes on to argue, one must handle God, the Bible, and hermeneutics together, as "first theology." What is Ryrie's approach and how does it affect his theological method?

Ryrie's "First Theology"

The organization of Ryrie's *Basic Theology*[71] would seem to point to the study of God, as Ryrie's first theology and the study of Bibliology and Hermeneutics as a close second. In the prolegomena section of his book, Ryrie, like Vanhoozer, declares a very close connection between the study of God and the study of the Scriptures: "The Trinitarian believes God is Triunity. That is a belief gleaned from the Bible. Therefore, he also believes the Bible to be true."[72] In the same section, Ryrie calls the

---

[70] Kevin J. Vanhoozer, *First Theology: God Scripture & Hermeneutics,* (Downers Grove, IL: InterVarsity, 2002), 16.

[71] The first section in Ryrie's *Basic Theology* following the prolegomena is the doctrine of God, and then the doctrine of Scripture.

[72] Charles C. Ryrie, *Basic Theology,* (Wheaton, IL: Victor, 1986), 16.

truthfulness of Scripture to be the "basic presupposition,"[73] which would argue for Bibliology as his "first theology." Ryrie states, "The theist believes there is a God. He mounts confirmatory evidence to support that belief, but basically he believes."[74] It is safe to say, that the study of God and the Bible in Ryrie's view must also be treated together. However a systematic theology book, by necessity, requires one to be treated first, accounting for the study of God voiced before Bibliology.

Ryrie's View of God

As stated previously, Ryrie presupposes that God exists as a triune God who has revealed Himself in the Scriptures. Although God is transcendent and not completely comprehensible, He has chosen to allow us to know Him, although not completely.[75] Ryrie believes, along with conservative evangelicals, that God has revealed Himself to all mankind through the conscience and through the requirements of the law written on their hearts. Ryrie also believes God has revealed His nature and purposes to man progressively in Scripture and through the use of language.[76] Ryrie adheres to the orthodox teachings regarding the person and nature of God.

Ryrie's View of the Bible

One's view of Scripture has a profound impact on one's theological method. Ryrie presupposes Scripture to be the inspired, inerrant word of God. He has complete confidence in

---

[73] Ryrie, *Basic Theology*, 16.
[74] Ryrie, *Basic Theology*.
[75] Ryrie, *Basic Theology*, 25.
[76] Ryrie, *Basic Theology*, 26–27.

the biblical record as absolute truth. In Ryrie's book on inerrancy, he seeks to harmonize Scripture, starting with the presupposition that it is without error, and all apparent contradictions can be explained. With this starting point, he is able to answer the attacks of errantists, who claim there are two contradictory accounts of creation, ask where Cain got his wife, point to contradictory accounts of Goliath's death, see contradictions in numbering, argue that the statements regarding the mustard seed are scientifically false, and argue for discrepancies regarding Judas's death. Ryrie concludes,

> Those represent passages currently being used as illustrations of errors...reasonable explanations are at hand. We need not conclude that errors are present in the text except for, possibly, occasional copyists' errors. How one views those suggestions will be a reflection of one's underlying confidence, or lack of it, in the Bible itself.[77]

Ryrie does not regard the copies of Scripture to be inerrant, just the original writings. Ryrie argues that "errancy feeds on itself. If all the words cannot be trusted, then one may tend not to do careful exegesis and therefore either ignore or refuse to accept a perfectly proper grammatical explanation... ."[78] Ryrie further states, "All of them [problem passages] do have reasonable explanations."[79] Elsewhere Ryrie states, "If someone comes to the Bible expecting or allowing for error, he can make a case for an errant Scripture. But if he comes expecting the

---

[77] Ryrie, *Basic Theology*, 88–89.
[78] Ryrie, *Basic Theology*, 94.
[79] Ryrie, *Basic Theology*, 100.

Bible to be inerrant, he can find plausible solutions, and even if he cannot honestly accept any of the suggested solutions, he can still believe that the Bible is inerrant and that we simply don't yet have enough facts to solve some of the problems."[80] Ryrie's view leaves room for the unknown, "You can believe there are errors, or you can believe that there would be perfect resolution if all the facts were known."[81] Ryrie's observations make clear the implications these foundational presuppositions have on one's interpretations and by de facto on one's theological method. Ryrie's theological method begins with a presupposition that the triune God of the Bible exists, and He has revealed Himself in the inspired, inerrant Scriptures.

Ryrie's Hermeneutic

It is not possible to overemphasize the importance of hermeneutics as it pertains to one's theological method. Ryrie's definition of Hermeneutics appears in typical Ryrie fashion— succinct and efficient: "the study of the principles of interpretation."[82] One's hermeneutic adopted and applied will by necessity affect one's theological method, and in turn one's interpretation. Therefore, it is helpful to first assess Ryrie's hermeneutical principles in understanding his theological method.

Historical-Grammatical Reading of Scripture

Ryrie consistently applies a literal hermeneutic in interpreting Scripture. Ryrie argues that this is the second *sine*

---

[80] Ryrie, *Basic Theology*, 98.
[81] Ryrie, *Basic Theology*, 99.
[82] Ryrie, *Basic Theology*, 110.

qua non of dispensationalism,[83] and is the basis for the distinction between Israel and the church.[84] This is often called the "historical-grammatical" hermeneutic. Other words used in place of literal are "normal" or "plain." Ryrie states, that it "might also be called plain interpretation so that no one receives the mistaken notion that the literal principle rules out figures of speech."[85] Ryrie argues for the plain reading of Scripture from the nature of God's revelation.

> God intended you to understand what the Bible teaches. This does not mean that you will comprehend all its truths at first reading or even in a lifetime, but it does mean that you can expect to learn a great deal. God used language which He meant to be taken just as normally and plainly as the words in this book.[86]

Ryrie consistently applies this same literal hermeneutic to the book of Revelation. He explains how a literal hermeneutic can allow for symbolism:

> The concept of a literal interpretation always raises questions since it seems to preclude anything symbolic, and the book obviously contains symbols. Perhaps saying "normal" or "plain" interpretation would be better than "literal," since futurists do recognize the presence of symbols in the book. The difference between the literalist

---

[83] Sine qua non is Latin, and has the idea of the essentials or things indispensible.

[84] Ryrie, *Basic Theology*, 40.

[85] Ryrie, *Basic Theology*, 80.

[86] Ryrie, *A Survey of Bible Doctrine* (Chicago: Moody Press, 1972), 9–10.

and the spiritualizer is simply that the former sees the symbols as conveying a plain meaning.[87]

In other words, every symbol has a literal referent, whereas the allegorizer/spiritualizer feels no impetus in finding a referent. Ryrie provides three rationales for a historical-grammatical hermeneutic. The first line of argumentation is regarding the nature of language:

> If God be the originator of language and if the chief purpose of originating it was to convey His message to humanity, then it must follow that He, being all-wise and all-loving, originated sufficient language to convey all that was in His heart to tell mankind. Furthermore, it must also follow that He would use language and expect people to understand it in its literal, normal, and plain sense. The Scriptures, then, cannot be regarded as an illustration of some special use of language so that in the interpretation of these Scriptures some deeper meaning of the words must be sought.[88]

Ryrie's second line of argumentation for a historical-grammatical hermeneutic rests on the example of fulfilled Old Testament prophecies. He argues that the prophecies concerning the birth, life, and death of Jesus Christ were fulfilled literally and precisely; therefore prophecies which have yet to be fulfilled should also follow this model.[89]

---

[87] Ryrie, *Revelation*, 9.
[88] Ryrie, *Dispensationalism*, 81.
[89] Ryrie, *Dispensationalism*, 81.

His third reason: it is the only means for objectivity. If the Scripture is not to be interpreted literally, then there can be as many interpretations as there are people.[90] In his view, dispensationalism is the by-product of the literal interpretation of Scripture and the dispensationalist is the most consistent in the application of the historical-grammatical hermeneutic. Ryrie states, "If literalism is the valid hermeneutical principle then that is an approach to the Scriptures which if consistently applied can only lead to dispensational theology."[91] Ryrie repeats, "As basic as one believes literal interpretation to be, to that extent he will of necessity become a dispensationalist."[92]

It does not take much investigation to find Ryrie's understanding of general hermeneutics or his consistent application of these rules to prophecy. In *The Basis of the Premillennial Faith,* Ryrie gives three general principles of interpretation. In *Basic Theology,* Ryrie adds a fourth.

1. *Interpret grammatically.* There is no more basic rule of interpretation than this. The interpreter must begin his work by studying the grammatical sense of the text, determining the exact meaning of the words according to the linguistic usage and connection.

2. *Interpret according to the context.* The Bible is not a book of words or verses put together without any relation to one another. Therefore, the context, which includes

---

[90] Ryrie, *Dispensationalism,* 82. These same three rationales are also articulated in Ryrie's *Basic Theology,* although arranged in a different order (*Basic Theology,* 113–114).

[91] Ryrie, "The Necessity of Dispensationalism," *Bibliotheca Sacra* 114, no. 455 (July 1957): 249.

[92] Ryrie, "The Necessity of Dispensationalism," 250.

both the immediate context and the wider scope of the section or book, must be studied in order to see the relation that each verse sustains to that which precedes and to that which follows.

3. *Compare Scripture with Scripture.* This principle of interpretation...not only uses parallel passages in Scripture but also regulates the interpretation of each passage in conformity with the whole tenor of revealed truth...The application of this principle of hermeneutics means the harmonization of Scripture. An obscure or seemingly contradictory passage cannot invalidate a doctrine clearly supported by this principle of the analogy of faith.[93]

4. *Recognize the progressiveness of revelation.* To be able to interpret plainly consistently, it is imperative to recognize that revelation was given progressively.[94]

Ryrie also clearly states what he believes to be the principles of interpretation that should govern the understanding of prophetic literature.

1. *Consistency in principle.* Prophecy is not a special case in that it demands special hermeneutics if such a system contradicts the basic principle of literal interpretation.

2. *Compare prophecy with prophecy.* Every prophecy is part of a wonderful scheme of revelation, and this entire

---

[93] Ryrie, *Basic Theology*, 36–37.
[94] Ryrie, *Basic Theology*, 114.

scheme as well as the interrelationship between the parts must be kept in mind.

3. *Interpretation differs from application.* Interpretation is one; application is manifold. The primary aim of the interpreter is, in every case to discover the true and only interpretation... there is a secondary application, but not interpretation."

4. *Figurative language...*the use of figurative language does not compromise or nullify the literal sense of the thing to which it is applied. Figures of speech are a legitimate grammatical usage for conveying a literal meaning.

5. *Law of fulfillment.* In the interpretation of unfulfilled prophecy, fulfilled prophecy forms the pattern... In other words look at how God has fulfilled prophecy in the past to see how He will in the future.

6. *Law of double fulfillment.* Often a prophecy may have a double fulfillment, one being in the immediate circumstances and another in the distant future.

7. *Law of time relationship.* Two or more events of a like character may be described in a common profile.[95]

In Ryrie's commentary on the book of Revelation he consistently adheres to the hermeneutical principles outlined

---

[95] Ryrie, *Basic Theology*, 40–45.

above. Concerning the fourth principle listed above, *figurative language*, he states, "The difference between the literalist and the spiritualizer is simply that the former sees the symbols as conveying a plain meaning."[96] And regarding his first principle, *consistency in principle*, he clarifies, "The futurist does not deny the presence of symbols in the book, nor does he claim to be able to explain every detail with certainty. But he does insist that the principle of plain interpretation be followed consistently throughout the book."[97]

It is significant to note that the principles outlined above are recorded in Ryrie's early writings,[98] yet he adhered to these principles of hermeneutics consistently throughout the body of his work. Ryrie's *Basic Theology* printed in 1986, although organized differently, is nearly the same in content. Ryrie's summary on the subject of hermeneutics is also a helpful conclusion to this discussion"

It is God who desired to give man His Word. It is God who also gave the gift of language so He could fulfill that desire. He gave us His Word in order to communicate, not confound. We should seek to understand that communication plainly, for that is the normal way beings communicate.[99]

Ryrie's historical-grammatical hermeneutic has a significant part to play in his theological method.

---

[96] Charles C. Ryrie, *Revelation* (Chicago: Moody Press, 1968), 9.

[97] Ryrie, *Revelation*, 10.

[98] The Basis of the Premillennial Faith, while printed in 1953, was based on his Th.D. dissertation at Dallas Theological Seminary.

[99] Ryrie, *Basic Theology*, 115.

Israel and the Church

It is not by accident that Ryrie's principles of hermeneutics were explored prior to investigating his understanding of Israel and the church. The hermeneutical principles articulated above will affect Ryrie's view regarding Israel. As indicated previously, one of Ryrie's three stated *sine qua non* of dispensationalism is a literal hermeneutic. A second *sine qua non* is maintaining a distinction between the church and Israel. Ryrie states, "The one who fails to distinguish Israel and the church consistently will inevitably not hold to dispensational distinctions; and one who does will."[100] Ryrie goes on to articulate his position regarding Israel. "Israel does not replace the church, they are two separate people groups with two clearly delineated purposes."[101] Ryrie also points out that this is not odd, for in fact God has a purpose for angels, a purpose for the nations that continue into the New Jerusalem, and even has a plan for those who reject Him.

In *The Basis of the Premillennial Faith,* Ryrie clarifies that a premillennialist interprets literally the promises made to Abraham and David and that those promises were (1) unconditional and (2) have, or will have, a future fulfillment.[102] Ryrie goes on to state, "In no sense have these promises made to Israel been abrogated or fulfilled by the church, which is a distinct body in this age having promises and a destiny different from Israel's."[103] Ryrie sees an inconsistency in how others see the church as replacing Israel. In his estimation, they do not consistently apply the rules of hermeneutics.

---

[100] Ryrie, *Dispensationalism*, 39.
[101] Ryrie, *Dispensationalism*, 39.
[102] Ryrie, *The Basis of the Premillennial Faith*, 12.
[103] Ryrie, *The Basis of the Premillennial Faith*, 12.

If one interprets literally, he arrives at the premillennial system...There is no disagreement over the fundamental rules of interpretation...the disagreement is in the interpretation of prophecy. The amillennialst's answer is special hermeneutics which are special in the sense that they contradict all regular hermeneutical principles. The premillennialist's answer includes some special considerations in interpreting prophecy...while at the same time being harmonious with the basic principles of hermeneutics.[104]

Ryrie also writes on the distinction between Israel and the church in his article "The Mystery in Ephesians 3." In this article, Ryrie makes a strong argument from the meaning of *mystery*. He begins by arguing that the classical Greek usage of the *musterion* is something that was hidden or was a secret.[105] He goes on to argue that the biblical usage is similar:

The idea of a mystery being something secret in Old Testament times but revealed in the New Testament is clearly seen in a passage like Colossians 1:26...Thus the concept of a mystery is basically a secret which only the initiated share. This includes two ideas: (1) a time when the secret was not known followed by a time when it became known; and (2) deeper or higher wisdom which is revealed to the one initiated into an understanding of the mystery... In other words, the mystery concerns Jews and Gentiles as joint-heirs, in a joint-body, and

[104] Ryrie, *The Basis of the Premillennial Faith*, 47.
[105] Charles C. Ryrie, "The Mystery in Ephesians 3," *Bibliotheca Sacra* 123, no. 439 (January 1966): 25.

joint-sharers of the promise in Christ. That the mystery contains the fact that Gentiles are included in God's plan of redemption is clear, and most non-dispensational writers stop at this point. But is this all there is to the mystery? If so, there is little mystery in that, for the Old Testament made this clear (Gen. 12:3; Isa. 42:6–7). If this is the mystery then Paul was wrong to label it a mystery, for it is neither something new nor some higher truth. The heart of the mystery is that there would be a "joint-body" for Jews and Gentiles.[106]

In the aforementioned article, Ryrie articulates the argument of the covenant theologian, who tries to point to the significance of the "as" in Ephesians 3:5 to indicate there was some revelation of the church in the Old Testament. Ryrie concisely and systematically defuses their argument by contending the following:

1. The parallel passage, Colossians 1:26, does not include the word "as" and unequivocally points to nothing being known in the Old Testament.

2. If "as" does show comparison, it does not necessarily follow that that the church was present in the Old Testament.

3. The Greek word "as" has several meanings.

---

[106] Ryrie, "The Mystery in Ephesians 3," 27.

4. One meaning that does not contradict, but rather harmonizes with Colossians 1:26, is the adjectival or declarative use, in which case the "as" clause would simply add additional information.[107]

After arguing for the distinction of Israel and the church on the basis of the meaning of "mystery," Ryrie proceeds to argue for the distinction on the basis of the beginning of the church as recorded in the book of Acts. Ryrie points out that even after Jesus' resurrection, He spoke of the church to be yet future.[108] Ryrie concludes, "Therefore the inescapable conclusion is that the body of Christ did not come into existence until the day of Pentecost when the first members of the body were joined to the risen Head...If by stretch of the interpretive imagination the body could be said to have existed before Pentecost, then it was without a head."[109]

Ryrie also argues for the distinction of the church from Israel on the basis of the "new man" in Ephesians.

That body-church is called a "new-man" (Eph. 2:15), not a continuation or remaking of Israel, but something new and distinct from the Israel of the Old Testament...Just as the redeemed before Abraham's day (like Enoch and Noah) were not a part of Israel, so the redeemed of this age are not either."[110]

---

[107] Ryrie, "The Mystery in Ephesians 3," 29.
[108] Ryrie, "The Mystery in Ephesians 3," 29.
[109] Ryrie, "The Mystery in Ephesians 3," 27–28.
[110] Ryrie, "The Mystery in Ephesians 3," 28.

There is no ambiguity in the writings of Ryrie. He consistently and regularly maintains that Israel and the church are two unique entities, with two unique plans and purposes of God.

Opposition to "Complementary Hermeneutics"

In recent years, theological and hermeneutical changes have taken place within some dispensational circles. This shifting has been labeled progressive dispensationalism. Their theological conclusions move the parties involved closer to the Covenant camp, and cause a blurring of the lines between Israel and the church. This shift has significant theological implications and is the result of adopting a new hermeneutic.

Progressive dispensationalists argue for "complementary hermeneutics," or what they might call an "enhancement" of biblical truth. According to them, "In making complementary additions... it does not jettison old promises. The enhancement is not at the expense of the original promise."[111] Ryrie is not satisfied with the progressive dispensationalists' theological conclusions or the hermeneutic upon which it is based. Ryrie argues that the complementary hermeneutic of the progressive dispensationalist "allows the New Testament to introduce changes and additions to Old Testament revelation."[112] He concludes that such a significant departure from the normal dispensational hermeneutic results in dispensationalists and even non-dispensationalists to rightly conclude that the progressive dispensationalist should no longer be classified as

---

[111] Craig A. Blaising and Darrell L. Bock, *Dispensationalism, Israel and the Church: The Search for Definition* (Grand Rapids: Zondervan, 1997), 392–393.

[112] Ryrie, *Dispensationalism*, 164.

dispensational.[113] This is the case if Ryrie's three *sine qua non* are legitimate definitive characteristics of dispensationalism. In Ryrie's view the "enhancement" of Old Testament revelation spoken of by the progressive dispensationalists equals a change of Old Testament revelation. If Christ is ruling on the throne of David currently, as the progressives contend, then the literal meaning and understanding of the original audience has been neglected and has been replaced by an "enhanced" meaning. The complementary hermeneutic, according to Ryrie, is an inconsistent one that incorporates a spiritualized meaning "here" along with the literal meaning "not yet."

Ryrie points out to his readers what he sees as the dangers of this view, "Are there limits on the use of a complementary hermeneutic, and, if so, how are these limits to be determined and by whom?"[114] His point is clear, the complementary hermeneutic results in the loss of objectivity. Ryrie's statement in *Basic Theology* is helpful: "If one does not employ normal interpretation, then objectivity is lost to the extent that he does not use it consistently... [This] results in different, inconsistent, and often contradictory interpretations."[115] Ryrie believes that the hermeneutic of the progressive dispensationalist has no limiting criteria to protect from the abuse of Scripture and violence committed to the Text.

Typology

Typology is an interesting, challenging subject with a wide-range of treatment. There are those who could be classified as "hyper-typers" who see types and anti-types in nearly every

---

[113] Ryrie, *Dispensationalism*, 162.
[114] Ryrie, *Dispensationalism*, 175.
[115] Ryrie, *Basic Theology*, 113.

object, person, and event in Scripture. Then there are those who will only acknowledge types expressly stated in the Scripture. Ryrie holds to a mediating position. He sees a type as, "a divinely purposed illustration which prefigures its corresponding reality." This definition not only covers types which are expressly designated so by the New Testament (e.g., 1 Cor. 10) but also allows for types not so designated (e.g., Joseph as a type of Christ)."[116] While Ryrie does not require that every type or anti-type be identified as such by the biblical authors, he does imply that there must be clear indicators in the text to point to it being "divinely purposed." In other words, a type cannot be determined arbitrarily. Ryrie points to the Feast of Pentecost as a good example of a type not expressly stated in Scripture, but the similarities cannot be overlooked and must have been divinely intended, "for although there is a clear type-antitype relationship, not all the details of the Old Testament feast find a corresponding reality in the events recorded in Acts 2."[117] Ryrie goes on to state,

> The phrase 'divinely purposed' should guard against an allegorical or pseudo-spiritual interpretation of types which sees chiefly the resemblances between Old Testament events and New Testament truths to the neglect of the historical geographical, and local parts of those events.[118]

---

[116] Ryrie, "The Significance of Pentecost," 330.
[117] Ryrie, "The Significance of Pentecost," 330.
[118] Ryrie, "The Significance of Pentecost," 330.

Ryrie's view prevents a too constrictive view of types, while at the same time, maintains criteria that avoids the excesses of a liberal treatment of types.

Ryrie consistently and judiciously applies the historical-grammatical hermeneutic to all of Scripture, including prophetic literature. These hermeneutical convictions are one of the key components of his theological method, and in his own words, "As basic as one believes literal interpretation to be, to that extent he will of necessity become a dispensationalist."[119] It is Ryrie's hermeneutic that leads him to be a dispensationalist. It causes him to see a distinction between Israel and the church. It results in his rejection of "complementary hermeneutics." It results in his careful handling of typology, and it influences virtually every interpretive decision he makes, including how to integrate the Old and New Testaments.

Ryrie's Integration of the Old and New Testament

How important is progressive revelation to interpretation? How do the New Testament authors use the Old Testament? How is one to interpret the covenants? One's answer to these questions demonstrates their integration of the Old and New Testaments.

Progressive Revelation

Ryrie explains that acknowledging progressive revelation is a recognition, "that God's message to man was not given in one single act but was unfolded in a series of successive acts and through the minds and hands of many men of varying backgrounds."[120] Ryrie maintains that the student of the Bible

---

[119] Ryrie, "The Significance of Pentecost," 250.
[120] Ryrie, *Dispensationalism*, 31.

must carefully observe the progressive nature of revelation. He contends that the dispensational perspective promotes a careful study of progressive revelation. In fact, only the dispensationalist does justice to progressive revelation in his view. He states, "Dispensationalism alone has a broad enough unifying principle to do justice to the unity of the progress of revelation on the one hand and the distinctiveness of the various stages in that progress on the other."[121] In a journal article entitled, "The Necessity of Dispensationalism," Ryrie points out what he sees as failures of covenant theology and accuracies of dispensational theology in handling accurately progressive revelation:

Covenant theology, then, because of the rigidity of its unifying principle of the covenant of grace can never show within its system proper progress of revelation. Dispensationalism, on the other hand, can and does give proper place to the idea of development. Under the various administrations of God different revelation was given to man, and that revelation was increasingly progressive in the scope of its content. Though similarities are present in various dispensations, they are part of a true development and not a result of employing the unifying principle of the covenant of grace. The particular manifestations of the will of God in each dispensation are given their full yet distinctive place in the progress of the revelation of God throughout the ages. Only dispensationalism can cause historical events and successions to be seen in their own light and not to be reflected in the artificial light of an overall covenant.

---

[121] Ryrie, *Dispensationalism*, 32.

Therefore, a correct philosophy of history with its requirements of a proper goal, a proper unifying principle, and a proper concept of progress is best satisfied by the dispensational system. Like the approach of Biblical distinctions, the approach through the proper concept of the philosophy of history leads to dispensationalism.[122]

According to Ryrie, progressive revelation does not mean that new revelation may completely change the meaning of something previously revealed, rather it brings additional understandings about God, His plans and purposes. Progressive revelation, "may add to it or even supersede it, but it does not contradict it."[123] Progressive revelation never changes the meaning of church, kingdom, or Israel. Each new dispensation has ingredients of newly and progressively revealed truth under which each person is responsible to operate.

The New Testament Authors' Use of the Old

How do the New Testament authors quote and illustrate from the Old Testament? This is a subject that is difficult and hotly debated. Ryrie makes a significant observation: "We must remember that most often the New Testament uses the Old Testament prophecies literally and does not spiritualize them."[124] Ryrie counts only seven examples "at most," which are spiritualized.[125] He goes on to say, "Hardly ever do New Testament writers not use the Old Testament in a historical-

---

[122] Ryrie, "The Necessity of Dispensationalism," 249.
[123] Ryrie, *Dispensationalism*, 81.
[124] Ryrie, *Basic Theology*, 115.
[125] Ryrie, *Basic Theology*, 115.

grammatical sense...The rule is that they interpreted the Old Testament plainly; the exceptions are rare and typological."[126] Ryrie believes, as do many other conservative scholars, that it was the prerogative of the apostles to do such. Since readers are not inspired by God, nor have apostolic authority, they cannot add new meaning to an Old Testament passage. Ryrie states,

> The Holy Spirit has the right to tell a New Testament writer to use an Old Testament quote with a different or new meaning. That does not give me the right to do that, because I am an interpreter not an author...You have to distinguish between what a writer of Scripture can do in his writing and what I cannot do in my interpretation.[127]

Ryrie finds the best explanation of the New Testament authors' use of the Old to be sourced in the inspiration of the Holy Spirit. He wisely reminds the interpreter that he has no such liberty.

The Abrahamic and Davidic Covenants

One's "First Theology," especially pertaining to one's hermeneutical presuppositions, will by necessity impact the discussion of the covenants found in Scripture. Is the Abrahamic Covenant eternal? Is it understood to be fulfilled spiritually, or should it be understood as a promise not yet realized, and therefore requiring a future fulfillment?

Ryrie's hermeneutical commitments lead him to conclude, that Abraham understood the promise of God to involve a literal land from the Nile to the Euphrates (Gen 15:19), a literal line of

---

[126] Ryrie, *Basic Theology*, 115.
[127] Ryrie, interview, November 9, 2012.

descendants, and a blessing upon and through his line. This covenant, in its plain understanding has not been fulfilled, and is not fulfilled in the church. One cannot take the New Testament and read it back into the Old Testament. This would be a contradiction of what the Abrahamic Covenant meant to its original readers, and it would do violence to the text. Ryrie states, "The Scriptures clearly teach that this is an eternal covenant based on the gracious promises of God. There may be delays, postponements, and chastisements, but an eternal covenant cannot, if God cannot deny Himself, be abrogated."[128] Ryrie believes that the Abrahamic Covenant is not conditional (as some covenant theologians say), nor is it spiritually received (as other covenant theologians argue). Ryrie makes a persuasive point, "Hundreds of years after Solomon's time the Scriptures still abound in promises concerning future possession of the land. This must prove that God and His prophets realized, whether the amillennialist does or not, that Solomon had not fulfilled the Abrahamic Covenant."[129]

The Davidic Covenant, according to Ryrie, is also an unconditional covenant which has yet to be inaugurated. It seems apparent to him and other classic dispensationalists that this is the case. Ryrie does not believe that Jesus has begun His reign in a spiritual way. In response to the progressive dispensationalist, Ryrie states,

The writer of Hebrews plainly declares that Christ "sat down at the right hand of the throne of God," not the throne of David (12:2). That does not deny that our Lord has all authority in heaven and earth or that He rules in

---

[128] Ryrie, *The Basis of the Premillennial Faith*, 53.
[129] Ryrie, *The Basis of the Premillennial Faith*, 61.

the world and in the church; rather, it denies that He is ruling on David's throne now and that the Davidic covenant has already been inaugurated. To conclude otherwise confuses the various rules in the Bible.[130]

Ryrie consistently applies his historical-grammatical hermeneutic to the Abrahamic and Davidic Covenants. He seeks to interpret literally and consistently, and interprets the text in light of how Abraham and David understood them in their original context. The New Testament does not reinterpret the Old Testament but rather helps to understand the implications of previous revelation. It builds upon it and clarifies it, and does not contradict it.

The Mosaic Covenant

While Ryrie understands the Abrahamic and Davidic Covenants to be unconditional and permanent, he finds good reason to interpret the Mosaic Covenant as conditional and temporary. Ryrie applies his historical-grammatical hermeneutic here as well. Concerning its conditional nature, he believes there were clear statements of contingency. If you do this,... you will be blessed; if you do that,... you will be cursed.

Concerning its temporal nature Ryrie states, "This passage [2 Corinthians 3:7–11] says that the Ten Commandments are a ministration of death; and furthermore, the same passage declares in no uncertain terms that they are done away (v.11)."[131] In his work on biblical theology, Ryrie writes, "The principal point of the writer is plain: these Jewish believers

---

[130] Ryrie, *Dispensationalism*, 169.
[131] Charles C. Ryrie, "The End of the Law," *Bibliotheca Sacra* 124, no. 495 (July 1967): 243–244.

[recipients of the book of Hebrews] were to look no longer to the Mosaic covenant with its services and priesthood, for now they had something better in Christ."[132] Yet, even with a plethora of statements speaking of the end of the law, some try to separate the Law into three parts and argue that the "moral law" is still in effect. He contends, "It is not uncommon in Christian theology to say that the judgments and ordinances are done away for the believer, but not the Decalogue. This is unscriptural, to say nothing of being illogical, in view of the unitized construction of the Law."[133] Ryrie argues for the entire Law being abrogated: "A cursory glance at the record of the giving of the law in the book of Exodus will show that the law was given to Israel as a unit."[134] Ryrie argues that it is one unit because (1) The Jews saw no distinction, (2) Exodus records the laws with no breaks between the Ten Commandments and the rest of the laws, (3) the commandments from each section were equally binding, and (4) because James says to break one of the laws is to violate all of them (James 2:10).

Once again, Ryrie consistently applies a historical-grammatical hermeneutic to the text, unhindered by theological baggage that accompanies many confessions or denominations established on the teachings of their respective founders (i.e. Calvin, Wesley, Luther). He allows the progressive revelation of the New Testament to give further insight into what the Old Testament had already predicted (Jeremiah 31).

---

[132] Ryrie, *Biblical Theology of the New Testament*, 248.

[133] Ryrie, *Biblical Theology of the New Testament*, 58.

[134] Charles C. Ryrie, *The Grace of God*, (Chicago: Moody Press, 1963), 57.

The New Covenant

The way one interprets the new covenant often shows the interpreter's theological presuppositions. It certainly shows his hermeneutical approach to the integration of the Old and New Testaments. Ryrie points out the amillennialist's interpretation of the book of Hebrews concerning the new covenant. The amillennialist believes the new covenant will be fulfilled by the church, despite the original promise in Jeremiah 31 being made with Israel, and "thereby obviating the need for a future millennial age."[135] Ryrie finds this interpretation unsatisfactory and an inconsistent use of the historical-grammatical hermeneutic.

Ryrie sees a need to accept the new covenant promise of Jeremiah 31 to be literally understood as the original readers would have interpreted it. In a footnote on Jeremiah 31 in his study Bible, he wrote about the new covenant: "It will be made in the future with the whole nation of Israel (Jer. 31:31); it will be unlike the Mosaic covenant in that it will be unconditional (Jer. 31:32); its provisions will include (1) a change of heart, (2) fellowship with God, (3) knowledge of the Lord, and (4) forgiveness of sins."[136]

We see that Ryrie is not willing to avert an Old Testament meaning with a supposed New Testament one. In his perspective, the New Testament has a priority over the Old Testament in that it helps to clarify and builds upon the incomplete Old Testament revelation, but it does not change it. It gives further details but does not controvert it. In his *Biblical Theology of the New Testament*, Ryrie lists three possible

---

[135] Ryrie, *Biblical Theology of the New Testament*, 249.

[136] Charles C. Ryrie, *The Ryrie Study Bible*, (Chicago: Moody, 1986), 1058.

interpretations held to by premillennialists, which do not require obviating the literal future earthly reign of Christ.[137] The three views on the New Covenant listed by Ryrie include: (1) the church receiving the blessings of the New Covenant with Israel, (2) the new covenant is with Israel only, but the church receives promises based on the blood of Christ, or (3) two New Covenants, one with Israel (yet future) and one with the church. At the time of the writing of his work on biblical theology in 1959, Ryrie held to the third view, "The new covenant under which the Church is blessed is not the same as that which Jeremiah promised for that is yet to be fulfilled to the house of Israel and the house of Judah as prophesied."[138] It appears that by 1986 Ryrie adopted a variation of the first or second view above, "Christ's blood is the basis of the new covenant (Matt. 26:28); Christians are ministers of it (2 Cor. 3:6); and it will yet have an aspect of its fulfillment in relation to Israel and Judah in the Millennium (as predicted in Jer. 31:31–34)."[139] What can be seen from these quotations and the body of Ryrie's work is that he desires to honestly grapple with the text, seeking to interpret the pertinent Scriptures in a way that maintains the authorial intent of both the New and Old Testament writers without obfuscating either of them.

Ryrie's Integration of Biblical Truth with Other Academic Disciplines Outside of the Bible

It is no secret that those who are scholars of the Bible and those who are experts in other disciplines often come to

---

[137] Ryrie, *Biblical Theology of the New Testament*, 249.

[138] Ryrie, *Biblical Theology of the New Testament*.

[139] This quotation is taken from the footnote of *The Ryrie Study Bible* on Hebrews 8:6, found on page 1675.

contradictory conclusions. How does one resolve these tensions? Ryrie gives some insightful thoughts on this subject.

Inspiration and Inerrancy of Scripture
In an interview with the writer of this paper, Ryrie puts his finger on what appears to be the source of the problem resulting in discrepancies between biblical scholars and experts of other disciplines.

> I think in the academic world, the attempt to integrate biblical truth with other disciplines is difficult and very often not successful... The reason is often because you cannot find the sociologist or psychologist or archeologist who has a knowledge of the Bible. He does not have time to be trained in the Bible like he does in his field.[140]

Ryrie proceeded to share an example of a college professor who had successfully integrated biblical truth into his secular teaching; the key to his success was that he knew the Bible almost as well as he understood biology. Unfortunately, this example seems to be the exception and not the norm.

When integrating the Bible with other disciplines, Ryrie's starting point is unashamedly the inspiration and inerrancy of Scripture. He has absolute confidence in the biblical record as absolute truth. In his own words, "If the Bible says something about [any given subject] than that is the standard."[141]

Others have a starting point that other "sciences" are truth and the Scripture must be interpreted in light of "scientific"

---

[140] Ryrie, interview, November 9, 2012.
[141] Ryrie, interview, November 9, 2012.

discoveries. Concerning the creation vs. theistic evolution debate, Ryrie articulates,

> Since the Bible and Christ Himself attest to the truthfulness of the account [creation story], since the Bible itself has been shown to be true in other areas (particularly in the matter of fulfilled prophecy), and since the data of the theory of evolution is built on circular arguments, is full of gaps, and requires an element of blind faith to believe, the choice of what to accept about creation should not be difficult.[142]

Later Ryrie states, "Although the Bible is not a textbook of science, when it records a scientific fact it speaks of that fact with infallible authority just the same as with matters of 'faith and practice'...One cannot hold to inspiration and infallibility of certain parts and not the inspiration of other parts."[143]

Ryrie's position can be summarized: the Scriptures are the only source of absolute truth and therefore any other "science" or other source of truth must be carefully interpreted in light of the Bible. Problems or contradictions can be explained, either as a misunderstanding of the text of Scripture or a faulty conclusion of the other sciences.

---

[142] Charles C. Ryrie, *Biblical Answers to Tough Questions*, (Fort Worth, TX: Tyndale Seminary, 2008), 141.

[143] Charles C. Ryrie, "The Importance of Inerrancy," in *Bibliotheca Sacra* (January 1963):141.

Dealing with Apparent Contradictions with Other Sources of Truth

Ryrie focuses an entire chapter in *Basic Theology* to address "problem passages." Here he starts from a perspective that the Bible is an inspired and inerrant book, and all apparent contradictions can be explained. If there is a "contradiction," there is an explanation, and it never is that the Bible is wrong. Concerning the question of the fossils of early men,

> It is the allegation of evolution that man is very old and that he has evolved from prior brute forms. In contrast the biblical account of creation insists that Adam and Eve were the first human beings, that they were sinless, that they subsequently sinned, and that the resultant effect on the entire race has been one of degeneration.[144]

Ryrie proceeds to question the fossil theory with skepticism, showing major problems in their theory: (1) the dating of fossil remains are based on circular reasoning, (2) the radiometric and fluorine methods of dating do not date the fossils absolutely, and (3) there is not one fossil record of intermediate forms to substantiate their theory.[145] Christians are often ridiculed for believing in Christianity and are accused of faith being their crutch. Ryrie states, "Seldom is creationism presented as a plausible explanation; rather it is portrayed [sic] as an emotional, unscientific, blind faith."[146] Ryrie goes on to reason that "science" also accepts some concepts by faith with no

---

[144] Charles C. Ryrie, "The Bible and Evolution," *Bibliotheca Sacra* 124, no. 493 (January 1967): 70.

[145] Ryrie, "The Bible and Evolution."

[146] Ryrie, "The Bible and Evolution," 72.

definitive proof: "The evidence of those who would explain life's origin on the basis of the accidental combination of suitable chemical elements is no more tangible than that of those people who place their faith in Divine Creation as the explanation of the development of life."[147]

Ryrie makes a strong and logical case for the biblical record and against the evolutionary hypothesis. He sees inspiration and inerrancy of Scripture as foundational to all investigation. He contends, "To acknowledge the divine-human authorship of the Bible resulting in its total inerrancy is analogous to the orthodox doctrine of the person of Christ."[148] Ryrie's point, the inspiration of Scripture is just as foundational to Christianity as the deity and humanity of Christ. The Bible is the only absolute standard and can be trusted. All other findings, all other sciences, must be subjected to theology the "queen of sciences."

Ryrie's Central Interpretive Motif (Unifying Principle)

Is it necessary for every theologian to have a central interpretive motif? Erickson argues in the affirmative, "Each theologian must decide on a particular theme which, for her or him, is the most significant and helpful in approaching theology as a whole."[149] While many theologians may find it helpful, a list of theologians could be supplied whose interpretive motif (if they have one) is indistinguishable. Finding an interpretive motif or unifying principle in Ryrie's writings would be most helpful in attempting to identify and explain Ryrie's theological method.

---

[147] Ryrie, "The Bible and Evolution."

[148] Charles C. Ryrie, "Important Aspects of Inerrancy," *Bibliotheca Sacra* 136, no. 541 (January 1979), 24.

[149] Millard Erickson, *Christian Theology*, 2nd ed. (Grand Rapids: Baker, 1998), 80.

There are certainly reoccurring themes and subject matters in the writings of Ryrie, but do they rise to the place of a unifying principle?

Grace

As developed in the section of this book entitled, *Ryrie, the Prolific Writer*, Charles Ryrie has written on a wide-range of subjects that cross over many different disciplines, and various target audiences. However, few subjects have been more developed than that of grace. Ryrie wrote an entire book called *The Grace of God*. The importance of the subject is seen in Ryrie's own words, "The concept of grace is the watershed that divides Roman Catholicism from Protestantism, Calvinism from Arminianism, modern liberalism from conservatism."[150] And again, "Christianity is distinct from all other religions because it is a message of grace. Jesus Christ is the supreme revelation of God's grace; salvation is by grace; and grace governs and empowers Christian living. Without grace Christianity is nothing."[151]

In addition to the book cited above, Ryrie has written a second book defending his view of grace, *So Great a Salvation*. Ryrie responds to the Lordship accusation that his view is "cheap grace." Ryrie argues that grace is not cheap rather it is expensive: "It is free to the recipient but costly to the donor."[152] The great significance of the subject of grace in the mind of Ryrie can be felt by his words:

---

[150] Ryrie, *The Grace of God*, 11.
[151] Ryrie, *The Grace of God*, 9.
[152] Ryrie, *So Great a Salvation*, 17.

What could I possibly offer that would help meet my
need? To offer the years of my life is to offer something
very imperfect and something which can do nothing to
forgive sin. To vow my willingness to change is to affirm
something I will not consistently keep; and even if I
could, it would not remove the guilt of my sin.[153]

Ryrie has given much time in his writings, interviews, and
lectures to discuss the ramifications of grace. Undoubtedly the
importance of this subject matter was impressed upon him by
his mentor, Chafer. In Ryrie's own words, "I was influenced on
his position and insistence on grace and grace alone."[154] If the
measure of a good teacher is passing on his views to his students,
Chafer was a success, and in turn Ryrie is too, for Ryrie has left
an indelible mark upon the countless men and women who sat
in his classroom, and countless individuals who have read his
works.

Ryrie also includes a section in his *Biblical Theology of the
New Testament*, with the title, "Biblical Theology Fosters a Deep
Appreciation of the Grace of God." In this section he argues that
the unfolding progressive revelation causes one "to stand in awe
of the fullness of God's grace, compared to that which was made
known in the Old Testament."[155]

Although the subject of grace is very important to Ryrie and
is found in many of his writings in one manner or another, it
does not impact all of his writings, nor does it tie all of his

---

[153] Ryrie, *So Great a Salvation*, 41.

[154] Ryrie, interview by the Evangelical Free Alliance,
http://vimeo.com/19816195, (accessed, November 15, 2012).

[155] Ryrie, *Biblical Theology of the New Testament*, 23.

writings together in a unifying way. For these reasons, the subject of grace falls short of his central motif.

God's Purpose: The Glory of God

The glory of God is a good candidate for Ryrie's interpretive motif. In *Dispensationalism* Ryrie criticizes the view of many covenant theologians, that the redemption of the elect is the unifying principle of human history. Ryrie gives three arguments against such a unifying principle: (1) Scripture itself points to the purpose of salvation as the glory of God; (2) all theologians recognize that God has plans for other created beings, not just humanity; (3) God's kingdom program, although it includes and requires the salvation of man, is not limited to it.[156] In other words, the redemption of the elect is too narrow of a unifying principle and incapable of including beings such as angels, or God's kingdom program. While not minimizing the importance of salvation, Ryrie states, it "is but one facet of the multifaceted diamond of the glory of God."[157]

In this same discussion, Ryrie seems to make his unifying principle clear, the glory of God,

> The dispensationalist sees a broader purpose in God's program for the world than salvation, and that purpose is His own glory. For the dispensationalist the glory of God is the governing principle and overall purpose, and the soteriological program is one of the principal means employed in bringing to pass the greatest demonstration of His own glory.[158]

---

[156] Ryrie, *Dispensationalism*, 94.
[157] Ryrie, *Dispensationalism*, 94.
[158] Ryrie, *Dispensationalism*, 93.

He makes a similar statement to the one cited above regarding the need to have a broader and more inclusive interpretive motif than covenant theology has, "for the dispensations reveal the glory of God as He manifests His character in the differing stewardships given to man."[159] Ryrie sees each dispensation as a means to bring about God's glory on earth.

God's Purpose for Human History: The Establishment of His Theocratic Kingdom

The glory of God, as articulated above, and in Ryrie's own words, appears to be his interpretive motif. He aptly argued that the salvation of mankind is too narrow of a primary purpose. Salvation of man is indeed too limited of a unifying principle. The glory of God is certainly a unifying principle. All creatures were created to bring glory to God. Scripture indicates that God is jealous and deserves all the praise and glory. However, the glory of God seems too broad of an interpretive motif. Using such a broad interpretive motif provides many interpretations of various passages of Scripture and has very few limiting implications. This writer contends that Ryrie's interpretive motif is the following: God's purpose for human history, the establishment of His theocratic kingdom. Ryrie's dispensational framework points to the culmination of human history in the theocratic kingdom; where man will finally accomplish God's intended purpose for him as indicated in Genesis 1:26–27. In Ryrie's words,

God does have various ways to manifest His glory, redemption being one—a principal one but not the only

---

[159] Ryrie, *Dispensationalism*, 94.

one. The various economies with their stewardship responsibilities are not so many compartments completely separated from each other but are stages in the progress of the revelation of the various ways in which God is glorified. And further, dispensationalism not only sees the various dispensations as successive manifestations of God's purpose but also as progressive manifestations of it. The entire program culminates, not in eternity but in history, in the millennial kingdom of the Lord Christ. This millennial culmination is the climax of history and the great goal of God's program for the ages.[160]

Movement towards the theocratic kingdom and its final culmination is indeed the heart of dispensationalism, and the focal point of so much of Ryrie's writing. It becomes the lens through which Ryrie sees and interprets Scripture as well as the course of events in human history. He states, "Dispensationalism sees the unity, the variety, and the progressiveness of this purpose of God for the world as no other system of theology."[161] Using one of Ryrie's routine tools of clarity is helpful at this point. In summary, it is best to see Ryrie's interpretive motif as God's purpose for human history, the establishment of His theocratic kingdom.

---

[160] Ryrie, *Dispensationalism*, 95.
[161] Ryrie, *Dispensationalism*, 95.

Ryrie's View of Related Disciplines within Biblical Studies

In his works, *Basic Theology* and *Biblical Theology of the New Testament*, Ryrie articulates the distinguishing markers of biblical, historical, and systematic theology as well as the significance of exegesis. In Ryrie's view all these disciplines are necessary and helpful, while he also articulates a priority and precedence in which they should occur.

Introductory Studies

Ryrie gives his readers a glimpse of his theological method and the order in which he believes the theological process ought to transpire. Ryrie begins with studies of introductory issues. He articulates,

> The results of the investigations of New Testament introduction are for the most part merely assumed and not reiterated in a work on Biblical Theology. However, since Biblical Theology cannot do without the critical investigations of introduction, the latter must precede the former, and to some extent must be included in it.[162]

Ryrie sees the importance of developing a solid understanding of these introductory issues because it is upon the foundation of these conclusions that exegesis and biblical theology is built.

Exegesis

According to Ryrie, out of all the disciplines mentioned above, exegesis and biblical theology have the closest connection because biblical theology builds immediately upon exegesis.[163] A

---

[162] Ryrie, *Biblical Theology of the New Testament*, 15.
[163] Ryrie, *Biblical Theology of the New Testament*, 16.

theologian who focuses on the task of biblical theology must give careful attention to the exegesis of Scripture. And exegesis must follow the historical-grammatical hermeneutic.

Biblical Theology

Ryrie contends biblical theology "deals systematically with the historically conditioned progress of the self-revelation of God in the Bible."[164] Ryrie breaks this definition into four parts: (1) as other areas of theology, biblical theology ought to be systematic, although not necessarily adhering to the same categories of systematic theology; (2) it involves the historic situation of the writer and the recipients, which compels him to write; (3) it studies the progressive nature of revelation; and (4) it finds its source in the Bible. Ryrie points out, "Strictly speaking Biblical Theology is foundational to Systematic Theology."[165] Biblical theology involves the investigation of parts of Scripture, a particular author's writings, or a particular period of time.

Systematic Theology

Ryrie notes that many do not understand the distinction between systematic and biblical theology.[166] Both should be systematic and both should be biblical. Ryrie gives a clear statement about the priority of theological disciplines in his view: "Logically and chronologically Biblical Theology should take precedence over Systematic Theology, for the order of study ought to be introduction, exegesis, historical backgrounds,

---

[164] Ryrie, *Basic Theology,* 14, and *Biblical Theology of the New Testament,* 12.

[165] Ryrie, *Biblical Theology of the New Testament,* 17.

[166] Ryrie, *Biblical Theology of the New Testament,* 17.

Biblical Theology, and finally Systematic Theology."[167] This statement is very significant as we evaluate Ryrie's theological method. Ryrie uses the illustration of a flower: biblical theology is the petals that make up the flower, and systematic theology is the blossom as a whole.[168] Systematic theology takes the work done in biblical theology, and correlates and systematizes it to understand what the complete cannon of Scripture says on a category of theology.

Historical Theology

Ryrie values historical theology. He sees it as an aid for students to better understand theology as a whole and avoid the mistakes of the past. He says it "focuses on what those who studied the Bible thought about its teachings either individually or collectively as in the pronouncements of church councils."[169] While Ryrie speaks of the significance of historical theology, no mention is given as to its place in the chronological order of the biblical disciplines.

A Summary of Ryrie's Theological Method

Erickson acknowledges that doing theology is an art and not just a science, and that rigidity in one's sequence cannot always be maintained.[170] However, after making such qualifications he clearly argues that a logical process is essential to doing theology: "Procedures need to be spelled out... there must be a... logical order of development."[171] Because Ryrie is a prolific

---

[167] Ryrie, *Biblical Theology of the New Testament*, 17.
[168] Ryrie, *Biblical Theology of the New Testament*, 18.
[169] Ryrie, *Basic Theology*, 13.
[170] Erickson, *Christian Theology*, 70.
[171] Erickson, *Christian Theology*, 70.

writer, much of his material is available for examination and his theological method can be determined. This writer's synthesis of Ryrie's theological method can be seen in Figure 1. Here is the precedence of the various logical and chronological steps within his theological method as perceived by this writer:

Presuppositions→Hermeneutics→Introductory Issues→Exegesis→Historical Backgrounds→Biblical Theology→ Historical Theology→Systematic Theology→Continued Theological Refinement

Figure 1: Priority and Sequence of Ryrie's Theological Method

Ryrie unashamedly begins with a set of presuppositions. Certainly many of these presuppositions were handed down to him from his father, Gaebelein, and Chafer, among others. But ultimately he came to embrace these presuppositions as his own. He presupposes the existence of God. He presupposes that God is the triune God of the Scripture and that this triune God has made Himself known to His creation through the special revelation recorded in Scripture. He also presupposes that the Scriptures are inspired and inerrant in the original autographs. Ryrie indicates that he does accrue "confirmatory evidence" to support his presuppositions, but ultimately he believes.[172]

Once acknowledging his presuppositions, developing a solid hermeneutic is the next step in Ryrie's theological method. As a

---

[172] Ryrie, *Basic Theology*, 16.

young boy, Ryrie was taught the historical-grammatical method, although he may not have been familiar with the term. His father passed on the teachings of Scofield and Chafer. Frank Gaebelein taught Charles Ryrie using a plain hermeneutic, and Ryrie heard the great preaching of the famous Presbyterian dispensationalist Donald Grey Barnhouse. Ryrie had a great theological pedigree upon which he advanced the cause of dispensationalism and the plain, normal, literal hermeneutic. Ryrie's theological method was profoundly impacted by his hermeneutical allegiances.

Investigating introductory issues is the third step in Ryrie's theological method. Although not much time is given to the subject of introductory issues in the writings of Ryrie, he understood the importance of studying introductory issues for a proper exegesis, biblical theology, and ultimately systematic theology of Scripture.

After a careful study of the introductory issues, Ryrie moves on to exegesis of passages of Scripture. He applies the historical-grammatical hermeneutic in his exegetical process. The product of this exegetical step is essential to his biblical theology.

The fifth step of Ryrie's theological method involves a study of historical backgrounds. This writer found nothing else stated concerning historical backgrounds or the rationale for its placement before biblical theology apart from the one quote referenced above.[173]

After doing an exegesis of the texts of Scripture and a study of the historical background, the sixth step in Ryrie's method is biblical theology. Here Ryrie takes all that is learned in his exegesis, and then studies the theology of particular authors

---

[173] Ryrie, *Biblical Theology of the New Testament*, 17.

and/or particular periods of time. This is done with an emphasis upon the progress of revelation.

It is not clear as to where historical theology should be placed in Ryrie's process. This writer chooses to place it before systematic theology as another tool to establishing good theological conclusions, but it could be placed afterwards to serve as a validation/check of his theological conclusions.

Systematic theology is nearly the final step. Taking all the exegesis and biblical theology through a solid hermeneutic, Ryrie then correlates and systematizes what the entire Bible has to say about various categories of theology.

The final step is theological refinement. The theologian should always be willing to go wherever the text leads. Every theologian should be continuously assessing his system and his understanding of Scripture in light of a greater and increasing knowledge and understanding of the text. This can be seen in the example cited previously regarding the new covenant.[174] Theological refinement should never stop. A theologian is always learning more and seeking to incorporate it into his theological understanding.

Charles Caldwell Ryrie is indeed one of the most influential theologians of the twentieth century. He has made a profound and world-wide impact on evangelicalism as a tenured professor and president, as a bold pioneer, as a prolific writer, as an ardent apologist, and as an ordained minister. He is known as a careful, consistent, and cautious interpreter of Scripture. He is an

---

[174] It appears that Ryrie came to one conclusion in 1959, at the time of the writing of his *Biblical Theology*, but after further study, contemplation, and as his knowledge of the Scripture increased, theological refinement took place in his understanding of the New Covenant as articulated in his study Bible and then again in pages 200–205 of *Dispensationalism*.

exegete that is honest with the text and humble in his presentation of it. His writing style contains great clarity and charity. And he is a theologian who is enamored by the grace of God, who desires for the glory of God to be known. For these reasons and more, Charles C. Ryrie's theological method is worthy of further investigation, consideration, and replication.

BIBLIOGRAPHY

Blaising, Craig A. and Darrell L. Bock, *Dispensationalism, Israel and the Church: The Search for Definition,* Grand Rapids: Zondervan, 1997.

Enns, Paul P. "Charles C. Ryrie," in *Dictionary of Premillennial Theology,* ed. Mal Couch, 67–70, Grand Rapids: Kregel Publications, 1996.

Enns, Paul P. "Charles C. Ryrie," in *Elwell's Handbook of Evangelical Theologians,* ed. Walter A. Elwell, Grand Rapids: Baker Publishing Group, 1993. In Logos Bible Software.

Erickson, Millard. *Christian Theology,* 2d ed. Grand Rapids: Baker Books, 1998.

Fawcett Cheryl L. and Jamie Thompson, "Frank E. Gaebelein," http://www2.talbot.edu/ce20/educators/view.cfm?n=frank _gaebelein#bibliography (accessed, 11/16/2012).

Goemaat Darrell, and Kevin Mungons. "Have Something to Say, and Say It Clearly: Q & A with Dr. Charles Ryrie," *Baptist Bulletin,* November, (2008): 27–30.

Hannah, John D. *An Uncommon Union: Dallas Theological Seminary and American Evangelicalism,* Grand Rapids:

Zondervan, 2009.

Mungons, Kevin. "Charles Ryrie on Sloppy Theology," *Baptist Bulletin,* www.baptistbulletin.org/?p=1296 (accessed 11/5/2012).

Ryrie, Charles C. interview by author, November 11, 2012 and November 16, 2012. Audio recording. Phone Conversation from Tóalmás Hungary, interviewee Dallas, TX.

Ryrie, Charles C. video interview, Evangelical Free Alliance, http://vimeo.com/19816195 (accessed 10/13/2012).

Ryrie, Charles Caldwell. *The Acts of the Apostles,* Chicago: Moody Press, 1961.

_____. *A Survey of Bible Doctrine,* Chicago: Moody Press, 1972.

_____. *Basic Theology,* Wheaton: Victor Books, 1986.

_____. *The Basis of the Premillennial Faith,* New York: Loizeaux Brothers, 1953.

_____. *The Best Is Yet to Come,* Chicago: Moody Press, 1981.

_____. "The Bible and Evolution," *Bibliotheca Sacra* January (1967): 66-78.

_____. *Biblical Theology of the New Testament,* Chicago: Moody Press, 1959.

_____. *Biblical Answers to Tough Questions,* np: Tyndale Seminary Press, 2008.

_____. *Come Quickly Lord Jesus: What You Need to Know About the Rapture,* Eugene, Oregon: Harvest House Publishers, 1996.

_____. *Dispensationalism,* Chicago: Moody Press, 1995.

_____. *Dispensationalism Today,* Chicago: Moody Press, 1965.

_____. "The End of the Law" *Bibliotheca Sacra* July (1967): 239–247.

_____. *The Final Countdown: God's blueprint for future events,* Wheaton: Victor Books, 1982.

_____. *The Grace of God,* Chicago: Moody Press, 1963.

_____. *The Holy Spirit,* Chicago: Moody Press, 1965.

_____. "Important Aspects of Inerrancy," *Bibliotheca Sacra* January (1979): 16–24

_____. "The Importance of Inerrancy," *Bibliotheca Sacra* January (1963): 137–144.

_____. *The Miracles of Our Lord,* Dubuque, Iowa: ECS Ministries, 2005.

_____. "The Mystery in Ephesians 3," *Bibliotheca Sacra* January

(1966): 24–31.

_____. "The Necessity of the Dispensationalism," *Bibliotheca Sacra* July (1957): 243–254.

_____. *Neo-Orthodoxy: What It Is and What It Does*, Chicago: Moody Press, 1956.

_____. "The Pauline Doctrine of the Church," *Bibliotheca Sacra* January (1958): 62–67.

_____. *Revelation*, Chicago: Moody Press, 1968.

_____. *The Role of Women in the Church*, 2nd ed, Nashville: B & H Publishing Group, 2011.

_____. *The Ryrie Study Bible*, Chicago: Moody Press, 1986.

_____. "The Significance of Pentecost," *Bibliotheca Sacra* October (1955): 330–339.

_____. *So Great a Salvation: What It Means to Believe In Jesus Christ*, Wheaton: Victor Books, 1989.

_____. "What is Spirituality," *Bibliotheca Sacra* July (1969): 204–213.

_____. *What You Should Know About Inerrancy*, Chicago: Moody Press, 1981.

Stallard, Michael D. *The Early Twentieth-Century Dispensationalism of Arno C. Gaebelein*, Lewiston, NY:

The Edwin Mellen Press, 2002.

Vanhoozer, Kevin J. *First Theology: God Scripture & Hermeneutics*, Downers Grove: InterVarsity Press, 2002.

Vincent, James *The MBI Story: The Vision and Worldwide Impact of Moody Bible Institute*, Chicago: Moody Publishers, 2011.

Anonymous, "Dr. Charles C. Ryrie" *This is Dallas*, v. 46, no. 1, (1970): 3–4.

Made in the USA
Coppell, TX
29 November 2022

87310388R00056